How to Make
Slime

Hands-On SCIENCE FUN

by Lori Shores

Consulting Editor: Gail Saunders-Smith, PhD

Consultant: Ronald Browne, PhD
Department of Elementary & Early Childhood Education
Minnesota State University, Mankato

CAPSTONE PRESS
a capstone imprint

Pebble Plus is published by Capstone Press,
151 Good Counsel Drive, P.O. Box 669, Mankato, Minnesota 56002.
www.capstonepub.com

032010
005740CGF10

Books published by Capstone Press are manufactured with paper
containing at least 10 percent post-consumer waste.

Library of Congress Cataloging-in-Publication Data
Shores, Lori.
    How to make slime / by Lori Shores.
    p. cm.—(Pebble plus. Hands-on science fun)
    Includes bibliographical references and index.
    Summary: "Simple text and full-color photos instruct readers on how to make slime and explain the science behind
the activity"—Provided by publisher.
    ISBN 978-1-4296-4492-1 (library binding)
    ISBN 978-1-4296-5575-0 (paperback)
    1. Plasticity—Juvenile literature. 2. Emulsions—Juvenile literature. 3. Cornstarch—Juvenile literature. I. Title. II.
Series.
TA418.14.S56 2011
620.1'1233—dc22   2009051420

Editorial Credits
Erika L. Shores, editor; Juliette Peters, designer; Sarah Schuette; photo studio specialist; Marcy Morin, scheduler;
    Eric Manske, production specialist

Photo Credits
Capstone Studio/Karon Dubke, all

Note to Parents and Teachers

The Hands-On Science Fun set supports national science standards related to physical
science. This book describes and illustrates making slime. The images support early readers
in understanding the text. The repetition of words and phrases helps early readers learn new
words. This book also introduces early readers to subject-specific vocabulary words, which are
defined in the Glossary section. Early readers may need assistance to read some words and to
use the Table of Contents, Glossary, Read More, Internet Sites, and Index sections of the book.

Table of Contents

Safety Note:
**Please ask an adult for help
when making slime.**

Getting Started

What's runny like glue,

but also hard like rubber?

Slime! It feels like a solid

and a liquid at the same time.

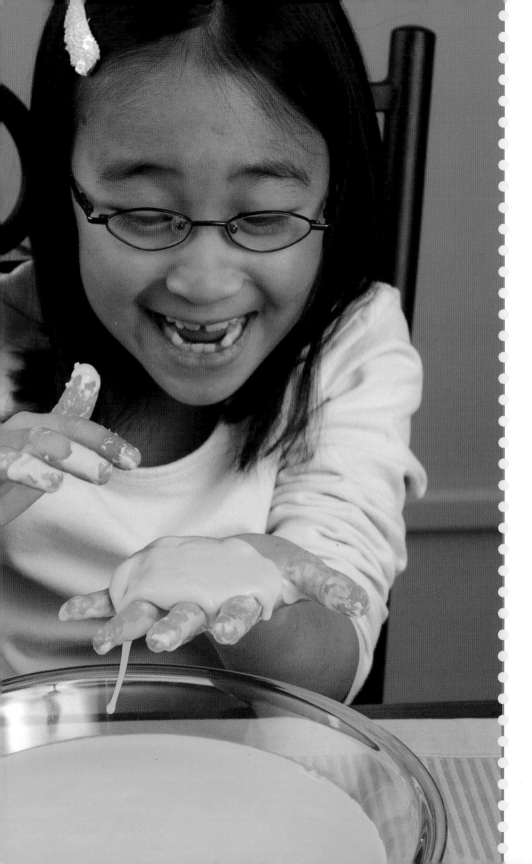

Here's what you need:

dish

food coloring

1 cup (240 mL)
cornstarch

spoon

½ cup (120 mL) water

Making Slime

Put ½ cup water
in a large dish.

Add a few drops
of green food coloring.

Add 1 cup of cornstarch

a little at a time.

Stir the mixture well

with a spoon.

The slime should tear
when stirred quickly.

If it doesn't tear, add
a little more cornstarch
one spoonful at a time.

Gently rest your hand
on top of the slime.

Then quickly slap
the surface of the slime.

What happens?

Try making a slime ball.

Push on it as you roll it
in your hands.

What happens when
you let go?

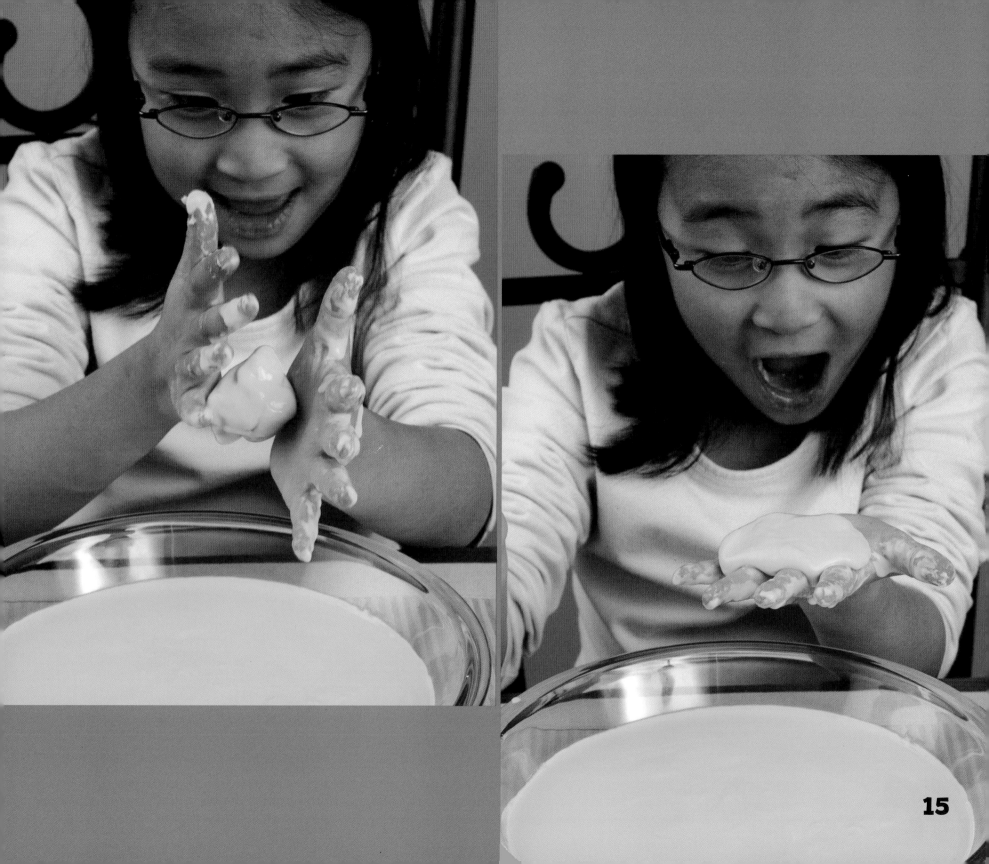

How Does It Work?

Water and cornstarch don't mix completely. The slime is mostly tightly packed bits of cornstarch. The water flows around those bits.

When your hand moves

slowly through the slime,

the cornstarch moves around.

The water flows and the slime

seems like a liquid.

When you slap the slime,
the cornstarch doesn't have time
to move. The water can't flow,
and the slime feels solid.

Glossary

cornstarch—a flour-like ingredient made from corn

liquid—a wet substance that can be poured

mixture—something made up of different things mixed together

rubber—a strong, elastic substance used to make items such as tires, balls, and boots

solid—a substance that holds its shape

surface—the top part of something

Read More

Oxlade, Chris. *Mixing and Separating.* Changing Materials. Chicago: Heinemann Library, 2009.

VanCleave, Janice Pratt. *Janice VanCleave's Big Book of Play and Find Out Science Projects.* New York: Jossey-Bass, 2007.

Internet Sites

FactHound offers a safe, fun way to find Internet sites related to this book. All of the sites on FactHound have been researched by our staff.

Here's all you do:

Visit *www.facthound.com*

FactHound will fetch the best sites for you!

Index

Word Count: 180
Grade: 1
Early-Intervention Level: 19

24

Norge